CONTENTS

WHAT IS A GOGO®?

As soon as you put a Gogo in your hand, you'll see why it is so original. Its face, shape and colouring are unique.

But there are lots more things you need to know about the Gogo's.

01 MOSH

Super kind. All the Gogo's want to be friends with Mosh.

SPECIAL ABILITY: **Magic Smile**

FAVOURITE GAME: K.O.

SKILLS:

NAME AND NUMBER

Every Gogo has a name and number. You'll find all their names in this handbook. If you look closely at the back of your Gogo, you'll find its number printed just above the MAGIC BOX INT. stamp.

GOGO PERSONALITIES

Each Gogo is very special and has its own personality and special abilities. If you want to know more about them, you can read their profiles right here in this handbook. You'll also find information on each of the Gogo's favourite games.

01 MOSH

Super kind. All the Gogo's want to be friends with Mosh.

SPECIAL ABILITY: **Magic Smile**

FAVOURITE GAME: **K.O.**

HOW TO PLAY?

You'll never be bored with a Gogo; there are so many games to play! Different Gogo's are better for playing different games depending on their size, shape and weight. Check out the profiles and use the handy guide to find out which games will best suit your Gogo's.

SKILLS:

SPEED: This shows whether the Gogo will gain speed and crash strength.

BOUNCE: This tells you whether it is easy to predict where the Gogo will land after it's thrown or whether it is likely to fly off in a direction you didn't expect.

BALANCE: This shows the likelihood of the Gogo standing up when it is thrown – remember a standing Gogo gets a much higher score.

COLOURS

Each Gogo is available in five different colours. All the colours of every Gogo can be found at the back of this handbook in the checklist section.

THE BACK

Look on the back of your Gogo's and you'll find they are all designed the same so that you can hold them or throw them with just one finger. Of course, practise is the key to becoming a Gogo champion.

DON'T ACCEPT ANY IMITATIONS

Pick up a Gogo and turn it over to check that it has the MAGIC BOX INT. stamp. The MAGIC BOX INT. stamp guarantees that your Gogo is an original, has a fantastic bounce and is a bright, shiny colour.

CRAZY BONES
THROUGH HISTORY

I'll bet you didn't know the Gogo's Crazy Bones you hold in your hand today have actually been around since before you were born. In fact they've been around since before anyone on this planet was born.

Children were playing their own version of Gogo's as far back as 330 BC in ancient Greece. In those days they didn't have cool characters like Skull and Mosh; in fact they used the bones of sheep. How gross is that?

The game was commonly known as Knucklebones, although they actually used the ankle bones because of their shape, which is very similar to some of the Gogo's we have today.

According to Greek mythology, the game was also played by soldiers during the epic Trojan War. Some ancient Greeks thought that the game was handed down to mortals by the god Zeus himself while ancient Egyptians believed it was invented by their god, Thoth.

Roman soldiers used to play something similar to the standard Gogo's game: points were scored depending on how the bones fell when thrown on the floor. Different scoring combinations were named after the various Roman gods: the highest was called Venus after the goddess of love. It was the favourite game of many Roman Centurions during their breaks from battle.

As far back as the 16th century children in Britain were playing a game called Fivestones using bones that they called hucklebones. Fivestones involved throwing one bone in the air and trying to pick up the bones on the floor before catching the falling one. The game eventually turned into the modern game of "Jacks" and the bones were replaced with metal pieces and a small ball.

Today we don't have to resort to using animal bones: we have great characters like Fist, Aiko and Matsue in a multitude of wonderful colours!

So next time you throw your Gogo's down, remember that people have been playing this game for hundreds of years!

01 MOSH

Super kind. All the Gogo's want to be friends with Mosh.

SPECIAL ABILITY: Magic Smile

FAVOURITE GAME: K.O.

SKILLS:

NASAKO 02

Always cool because he has a special scoring technique.

SPECIAL ABILITY: Double Fast Hook

FAVOURITE GAME: Battle

SKILLS:

PROFILES

SATO 03

♂

Ready for the fight.
Where's the ring?

SPECIAL ABILITY:
K.O. Punch

FAVOURITE GAME: Battle

SKILLS:

04 OKORI

♂

Nobody knows what he eats,
but whatever it is,
it isn't doing him any good.

SPECIAL ABILITY:
Eating

FAVOURITE GAME: Scoring

SKILLS:

PROFILES

TORI 05

Clever and fun,
he likes to be the boss.

SPECIAL ABILITY:
Jumps Walls

FAVOURITE GAME: Scoring

SKILLS:

06 HELLY

The fastest Gogo.
His helmet helps him to go
breathtakingly fast.

SPECIAL ABILITY:
Continuous Sprint

FAVOURITE GAME: On Line

SKILLS:

PROFILES

SKULL 07

He looks mysterious and when you least expect it, he'll do something funny to make you jump.

SPECIAL ABILITY:
Spooky Skills

FAVOURITE GAME: Basket

SKILLS:

08 + 08 S

ANGIRU

Tell Angiru your secrets and they will be safe for ever.

SPECIAL ABILITY:
Keeps Secrets

FAVOURITE GAME: Basket

SKILLS:

PROFILES

UMU 09

Likes to visit the swimming pool every day to think up new ideas.

SPECIAL ABILITY:
Intelligent Swimming

FAVOURITE GAME: In Flight

SKILLS:

AIKO 10

The Gogo with the best sense of smell. Can detect a smell from a mile away.

SPECIAL ABILITY:
Wonder Nose

FAVOURITE GAME: In Flight

SKILLS:

PROFILES

ICHIRO

Don't stare into its eyes. You'll be overcome by its great mental power.

SPECIAL ABILITY: Dagger Eyes

FAVOURITE GAME: Bowling

SKILLS:

12 NUCLOS

Absorbs pollution and leaves the air really clean.

SPECIAL ABILITY: Pollution Reduction

FAVOURITE GAME: K.O.

SKILLS:

13 BOY ♂

The best blindfolded runner.
He never falls over.

SPECIAL ABILITY:
Sensory Space Radar

FAVOURITE GAME: **Basket**

SKILLS:

NEKO 14 ♂

Uses his body to protect the
other Gogo's from fire.

SPECIAL ABILITY:
Flame Catcher

FAVOURITE GAME: **On Line**

SKILLS:

PROFILES

15 HAZARD

When faced with danger, it just grits its teeth and carries on.

SPECIAL ABILITY: Courage

FAVOURITE GAME: K.O.

SKILLS:

16 SUN

Fires a ray of optimism at every Gogo in it's path.

SPECIAL ABILITY: Happy Ray

FAVOURITE GAME: K.O.

SKILLS:

GAME RULES

SCORING

1 Players choose the number of Gogo's to be used. This can be anything from one to five Gogo's at a time.

2 Each player takes turns to throw their Gogo's on the floor.

3 Using the chart below, work out your score by looking at how the Gogo's land.

GO GO CRAZY!!

SCORE CHART

| 5 POINTS | 2 POINTS | 1 POINTS | 0 POINTS |

4 Each player has three goes and the one with the highest score at the end wins.
Of course, you can take more turns if you are looking for a longer game!

GAME RULES

BATTLE

1 Two players arrange six or more of their Gogo's in parallel rows a short distance apart.

2 Players must decide before the start of the match how many throws there will be.

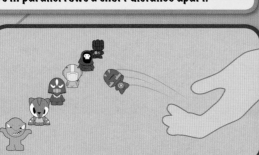

3 Players then throw their Gogo at their opponent's row and attempt to knock Gogo's out of the line.

TIPS

If using basic rules, the Gogo's do not need to fall over completely, but simply be knocked out of the line.

If you want to play advanced rules, then the Gogo's must actually be knocked over as well as being pushed out of the line.

4 The player who knocks down the most of their opponent's Gogo's wins.

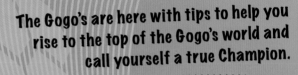

TIPS FROM

If you want to be a Gogo's Grand Champion and the envy of all your friends, you are going to need to practise.

The Gogo's are here with tips to help you rise to the top of the Gogo's world and call yourself a true Champion.

When using small Gogo's like me, flicking the bottom will give you height. Flicking at my head will make me go faster but I'm less likely to land on my feet.

Never use a lightweight Gogo when playing Battle as it will not travel very far when flicked and will knock over less Gogo's when it hits.

For greater accuracy, always try to flick directly at the **MAGIC BOX INT.** logo on the back of your Gogo.

THE CHAMPS

When playing Battle, move your Gogo just right of centre and flick the right-hand side. This will make it fly to the left and give you more chance of hitting multiple Gogo's. You can use this tactic by flicking the left-hand side to send the Gogo to the right.

Use small and narrow Gogo's like me for your line-up in Battle as we are harder to hit. Remember to use a chunky Gogo for shooting, though, as it will do more damage.

Do your Gogo's keep getting knocked over? Use someone like me and you'll be almost impossible to beat.

GAME RULES

BASEBALL

1 Draw a baseball diamond on the ground. Decide who will be 'batter' and place that player's Gogo on the batting plate.

2 That player then rolls four Gogo's and works out how far to move their Gogo using the score card below.

3 The player moves the Gogo's around the diamond the required number of spaces. Each time a Gogo makes a complete circuit of the diamond the player scores a point.

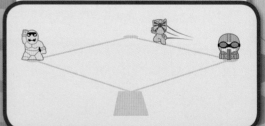

SCORE CARD

X1	HOME RUN	=	1 POINT
X4	HOME RUN	=	1 POINT
X3	TRIPLE	=	MOVE 3 BASES
X2	DOUBLE	=	MOVE 2 BASES
X1	SINGLE	=	MOVE 1 BASE
X0	ZERO	=	BATTER IS OUT!

4 When the batter is out three times it is the other player's turn. The game can go on for any number of rounds, but the traditional number for a baseball game is nine. The winner is the player with the most points at the end of the game.

GAME RULES

1 Using a piece of chalk, mark a circle or square on the floor.

2 Each player must place the same number of Gogo's inside the circle. Decide on the number of throws each player will get.

3 Players take turns to stand two metres away and throw a Gogo into the circle in an attempt to knock their opponent's Gogo's out of the circle.

4 If a Gogo gets knocked over but not completely out of the circle it can be put back into position, even if it falls on the line.

5 The winner is the player with the most Gogo's left in the circle at the end of the agreed number of throws.

PUZZLE CRAZY! JIGSAW JUMBLE

Can you complete this jigsaw?
Take a look at the pieces littered around
the board and see if you can tell which ones finish the jigsaw.
Not all of them will fit, so make sure you pick the right ones.

TUBE'S TRIVIA

1 Can you name the two Gogo's who have got into a bit of a mix-up here?

A.

B.

2 What is Nasako's special ability?

A. Single Slow Poke ◯

B. Double Fast Hook ◯

C. Magic Smile ◯

3 He's a daring pirate, also available in a special edition, who is he?

A. Hiraku ◯

B. Iman ◯

C. Gaiji ◯

4 On which Gogo would you find this symbol?

5 Can you untangle the name of the Gogo below?

Y N U R A S

◯ ◯ ◯ ◯ ◯ ◯

FIND ALL THE ANSWERS ON PAGE 88

HIRO 17

Solves problems with
electrifying 500W ideas.

SPECIAL ABILITY:
Electric Ideas

FAVOURITE GAME: In Flight

SKILLS:

18 AKA

Can collide with
100 Gogo's without getting
any bumps or bruises.

SPECIAL ABILITY:
Hammer Head

FAVOURITE GAME: Bowling

SKILLS:

PROFILES

MOLLY 19

Getting angry is no problem because it lasts less than a second.

SPECIAL ABILITY: Micro-Anger

FAVOURITE GAME: K.O.

SKILLS:

NARI 20

Don't try to stare out Nari - you will lose.

SPECIAL ABILITY: Concentration

FAVOURITE GAME: In Flight

SKILLS:

PROFILES

21 SIMI

Smiling charges up his powers.
He smiles and then shoots away.

SPECIAL ABILITY:
Power Smiles

FAVOURITE GAME: Battle

SKILLS:

CODI 22

Always connected.
Ask it anything and the data
will be downloaded.

SPECIAL ABILITY:
Quick Connection

FAVOURITE GAME: In Flight

SKILLS:

PROFILES

23 + 23 S

HIRAKU ♂

The most daring pirate – endless adventures.

SPECIAL ABILITY:
Boarding

FAVOURITE GAME: Bowling

SKILLS:

RUFUS 24 ♂

Sees things others can't using the powers of Planet X.

SPECIAL ABILITY:
X-Vision

FAVOURITE GAME: In Flight

SKILLS:

PROFILES

TEMP 25

Is the water really cold?
What time is it going to rain?
Just ask Temp.

SPECIAL ABILITY:
Weather Forecasting

FAVOURITE GAME: On Line

SKILLS:

PIBI 26

Organizes ideas in both sides
of its head. Need ideas,
speak to Pibi.

SPECIAL ABILITY:
Double Brain

FAVOURITE GAME: Basket

SKILLS:

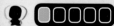

PROFILES

gogo's
CRAZY BONES

27 DARE

The best-looking Gogo.
He always looks his best.

SPECIAL ABILITY :
Photogenic

FAVOURITE GAME: Battle

SKILLS:

DANKO 28

Feline, fast, agile and
well behaved.

SPECIAL ABILITY :
Cute and Cuddly

FAVOURITE GAME: Bowling

SKILLS:

29 MC TOY ♂

Always careful and questioning.
Never makes a wrong move.

SPECIAL ABILITY:
No Mistakes

FAVOURITE GAME: In Flight

SKILLS:

30 GAIJI ♂

Takes control of the situation.
An expert in crowd control.

SPECIAL ABILITY:
Battle Helmet

FAVOURITE GAME: Battle

SKILLS:

31 LESSI ♂

Sometimes feels a little low.
You might need to perk him up.

SPECIAL ABILITY:
Shock-Absorber

FAVOURITE GAME: K.O.

SKILLS:

♂ POP 32 ♂

Loves music and dances
non-stop.

SPECIAL ABILITY:
Top Rhythm

FAVOURITE GAME: On Line

SKILLS:

GAME RULES

In flight

1 Players decide before starting how many rounds will be played. Place four Gogo's on the floor in a square shape and place a fifth one in the middle.

2 Take the Gogo from the middle and throw it into the air. Now try to pick up as many of the other Gogo's as you can before catching the Gogo you threw.

3 You must throw and catch the Gogo with the same hand you used to pick up the other Gogo's.

4 If the player doesn't catch the Gogo they threw up into the air, then no points are scored. Players get a point for every Gogo they pick up and the winner is the player with the most points at the end of all the rounds.

GAME RULES

Basket

1 Take a small cardboard or plastic box.

2 Decide how far from the players the box should be.

3 Each player picks five Gogo's of the same colour.

4 Take it in turns to throw a Gogo into the box, making sure it bounces before it goes in.

5 The player who gets the most Gogo's into the box is the winner.

PUZZLE CRAZY! PHOTO FOUL-UP

Something has gone wrong at the Gogo's photography studio and it's up to you to sort it out.

Can you spot the 10 differences between these two pictures. Make sure you get them right or the Gogo's will not be happy when they get the wrong picture back.

WACKY WORDS

Can you find the Gogo's hidden in this jumble of letters? Use the list to help you find all the Gogo's names.

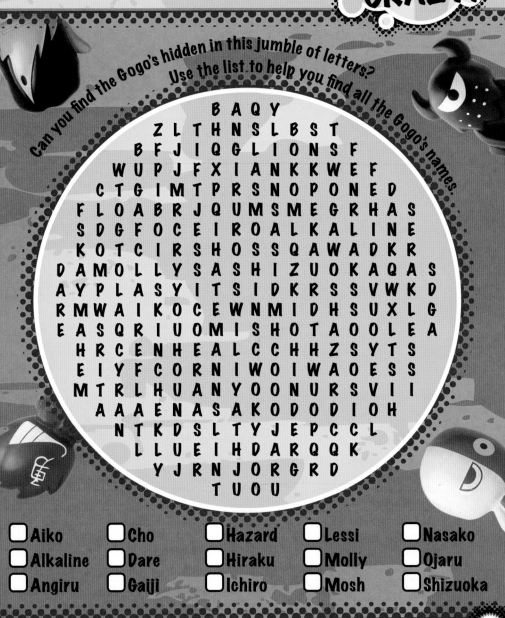

```
            B A Q Y
        Z L T H N S L B S T
      B F J I Q G L I O N S F
     W U P J F X I A N K K W E F
    C T G I M T P R S N O P O N E D
   F L O A B R J Q U M S M E G R H A S
   S D G F O C E I R O A L K A L I N E
   K O T C I R S H O S S Q A W A D K R
  D A M O L L Y S A S H I Z U O K A Q A S
  A Y P L A S Y I T S I D K R S S V W K D
  R M W A I K O C E W N M I D H S U X L G
  E A S Q R I U O M I S H O T A O O L E A
  H R C E N H E A L C C H H Z S Y T S
  E I Y F C O R N I W O I W A O E S S
  M T R L H U A N Y O O N U R S V I I
   A A A E N A S A K O D O D I O H
    N T K D S L T Y J E P C C L
    L L U E I H D A R Q Q K
     Y J R N J O R G R D
         T U O U
```

- ☐ Aiko
- ☐ Alkaline
- ☐ Angiru
- ☐ Cho
- ☐ Dare
- ☐ Gaiji
- ☐ Hazard
- ☐ Hiraku
- ☐ Ichiro
- ☐ Lessi
- ☐ Molly
- ☐ Mosh
- ☐ Nasako
- ☐ Ojaru
- ☐ Shizuoka

FIND ALL THE ANSWERS ON PAGE 89

GAME RULES

on line

1 Use any line on the ground or draw one yourself. Each player throws a Gogo without dragging it.

2 The player who manages to throw their Gogo nearest the line wins the throw.

3 If a player manages to get a Gogo directly on the line they score double points.

4 The player who wins the most throws wins the game.

GAME RULES

BOWLING

1 Each player must place the same number of Gogo's on the floor, about a hand width (with fingers spread) from the wall.

2 Take it in turns to throw a Gogo and knock over as many of your opponent's Gogo's as you can.

3 It doesn't matter if you knock down one of your own Gogo's: stand it up and carry on with the game. The player who knocks down the greatest number of their opponent's Gogo's wins the game.

TIPS FROM

If you want to be a Gogo's Grand Champion and the envy of all your friends, you are going to need to practise.

The Gogo's are here with tips to help you rise to the top of the Gogo's world and call yourself a true Champion.

Shooting with your finger on the side will give you greater accuracy. Flicking at the head with your finger vertical will give you greater height and distance.

If you want to make your Gogo fly like a rocket at its target, use a Gogo with a narrow head and wide base like me.

When playing games such as Bowling, where you need to roll your Gogo in a straight line, use round characters like me.

THE CHAMPS

When playing K.O. use wide Gogo's like me, Alkaline and Raysun. Our wider heads and bodies give you a better chance of knocking other Gogo's out.

If you want your Gogo's to land standing up and score maximum points, use Gogo's like me with a wide, heavy bases.

When playing games that need accuracy and control, use a large rounded Gogo such as Lessi, Kolo or me.

PROFILES

33 IMON

Absorbs ideas through its star.

SPECIAL ABILITY:
Mental Strength

FAVOURITE GAME: Battle

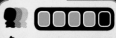

SKILLS:

JELLY 34

Brave enough for any battle.

SPECIAL ABILITY:
Super Warrior

FAVOURITE GAME: Battle

SKILLS:

PROFILES

SUMON 35

Traps his enemies inside his huge powerful jaws.

SPECIAL ABILITY:
Mouth-Cage

FAVOURITE GAME: **Bowling**

SKILLS:

36 CHO

Races ahead at full speed
- that's why he doesn't have
any teeth left.

SPECIAL ABILITY:
Energy

FAVOURITE GAME: **Battle**

SKILLS:

RAYSUN 37

Has a great time bringing
sunshine into the Gogo's world.

SPECIAL ABILITY:
Sun Ray

FAVOURITE GAME: **Bowling**

SKILLS:

38 + 38 S

FIST

Holds a secret strength
inside his fist.

SPECIAL ABILITY:
Ultimate Grip

FAVOURITE GAME: **Basket**

SKILLS:

PROFILES

ZAR-ZAR 39

Pretends not to understand but knows much more than you think.

SPECIAL ABILITY:
Cunning

FAVOURITE GAME: Basket

SKILLS:

40 HAYATO

Wants 20 mirrors nearby to keep an eye on everything.

SPECIAL ABILITY:
Super Wink

FAVOURITE GAME: Basket

SKILLS:

PROFILES

BIGU 41

Stands tall and upright.
Gives fun orders to the troops.

SPECIAL ABILITY:
Fun Orders

FAVOURITE GAME: **K.O.**

SKILLS:

OJARU 42

Badly sewn together
but strong enough to know
the secret of flight.

SPECIAL ABILITY:
Flying Ears

FAVOURITE GAME: **In Flight**

SKILLS:

PROFILES

43 SPEED

Turns his head with supersonic speed and always sees the world around him.

SPECIAL ABILITY: Panoramic View

FAVOURITE GAME: On Line

SKILLS:

44 TREMI

Appearances can be deceptive. Not as grumpy as he looks.

SPECIAL ABILITY: Laughter Mask

FAVOURITE GAME: Battle

SKILLS:

PROFILES

45 + 45 S

B-BOY ♂

Eats a lot of popcorn to improve his bouncing power.

SPECIAL ABILITY:
Popcorn Attack

FAVOURITE GAME: Basket

SKILLS:

MOCHI 46 ♂

A lucky charm amongst the Gogo's family.

SPECIAL ABILITY:
Lucky Power

FAVOURITE GAME: On Line

SKILLS:

POPUS 47

Digs long tunnels to move around without anyone knowing he is there.

SPECIAL ABILITY:
Earth Eater

FAVOURITE GAME: **Bowling**

SKILLS:

48 TUBE

Thanks to gramophone ears, it hears everything and can play it all back.

SPECIAL ABILITY:
Rec and Play

FAVOURITE GAME: **On Line**

SKILLS:

LOST GOGO'S®

When not bouncing around playing their favourite games, the Gogo's like a bit of relaxation. Can you help each of the hard-working Gogo's find the way to their favourite hobby?

TUBE'S TRIVIA

1 Can you untangle the name of the Gogo below?

2 Which of these Gogo's is not available in a special edition?

A. Fist

B. Cubic

C. B-Boy

3 On which Gogo would you find this symbol?

4 Can you name the two Gogo's who have got into a bit of a mix-up here?

A.

B.

5 Which Gogo sometimes needs perking up?

A. Dare

B. Lessi

C. Danko

FIND ALL THE ANSWERS ON PAGE 89

GAME RULES

Bone Flip

1 Before you start, players must decide how many rounds they want to play.

2 The first player places three Gogo's in the palm of their hand, then throws them up into the air a short distance.

3 While the Gogo's are in the air, the player flips their hand over and tries to catch as many Gogo's as they can on the back of their hand. A point is scored for each Gogo successfully caught.

4 The next player takes their turn and this completes one round. Add another Gogo for each round that is played.

5 The winner is the player with the most points at the end of all the rounds.

GAME RULES

CRAZY TOUCH

1 Take a box – a shoebox will do – and place at least ten Gogo's inside.

2 Each player takes it in turns to reach into the box with their eyes covered and pick up a Gogo.

3 With their eyes still covered, the player must guess which Gogo they have in their hand by feeling it. A correct guess scores a point. The first player to get ten points wins.

TIP

If you want to make the game even more difficult, the first player to get ten points in a row wins.

4 Give the box a shake between turns to mix the Gogo's up.

MAKE A GOGO'S

There has been a terrible mix-up at the Gogo's factory and the latest batch of Gogo's Crazy Bones© have had a bit of an accident.

Can you help out the Gogo's staff by finishing off these Gogo's designs? This is your chance to design your own Gogo. We've started you off with one, so get those pencils out and get Gogo-ing!

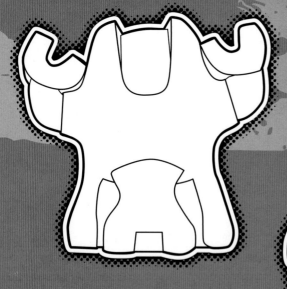

CRAZY BONE®!

GAME RULES

Hand Bone

1 Each player takes a number of Gogo's in their hand without letting the other player see how many.

2 With their hands closed, each player tries to guess how many Gogo's the other player has in their hand.

3 If you guess correctly that your opponent has three Gogo's in their hand, then you win three points. If you guess incorrectly, then you lose three points (or points equal to the number of Gogo's in their hand).

4 The winner is the first player to reach a score of 20.

TIP

Expert players can try to guess not only the number but also which Gogo's the other player has in their hand.

TUBE'S TRIVIA

1 Which of the following Gogo's does not like playing Battle?

A. Sato ⬭

B. Simi ⬭

C. Codi ⬭

2 Can you untangle the name of the Gogo below?

E S A U T M
⬭ ⬭ ⬭ ⬭ ⬭ ⬭

3 On which Gogo would you find this symbol?

4 Which Gogo would you find wearing this hat?

5 What is Kami Kami's special ability?

A. Graffiti-Flash ⬭

B. Super Bite ⬭

C. Double Brain ⬭

FIND ALL THE ANSWERS ON PAGE 90

PROFILES

CUBIC 49

A robot Gogo who is an expert mechanic.

SPECIAL ABILITY: Repairs Everything

FAVOURITE GAME: K.O.

SKILLS:

B-KING 50

When he sits down to think, he acts like a tribal chief.

SPECIAL ABILITY: Magic Horns

FAVOURITE GAME: Battle

SKILLS:

PROFILES

CROC 51

Croc is a chequered crocodile. In other words, a crocodile chess master.

SPECIAL ABILITY:
Check Mate

FAVOURITE GAME: Scoring

SKILLS:

52 UFUS

With its rubber Ninja body, it can fly long distances between bounces.

SPECIAL ABILITY:
Flying Bounce

FAVOURITE GAME: Scoring

SKILLS:

53 EGBOT

Communicates through waves, thanks to its electromagnetic mouth.

SPECIAL ABILITY:
Electric Jump

FAVOURITE GAME: **Basket**

SKILLS:

H-83 54

A strong shell makes it super resistant.

SPECIAL ABILITY:
Throws Stars

FAVOURITE GAME: **K.O.**

SKILLS:

ATORI 55

Keeps all its knowledge safe
inside and then closes the zip.

SPECIAL ABILITY:
Giga Memory

FAVOURITE GAME: **K.O.**

SKILLS:

B-BALL 56

If the sport has a ball,
he is the master.

SPECIAL ABILITY:
Ball Skills

FAVOURITE GAME: **Basket**

SKILLS:

PROFILES

USUZI 57

If something goes wrong, he is very nervous until a solution is found.

SPECIAL ABILITY: Clamp Click

FAVOURITE GAME: Battle

SKILLS:

58 ECO

Can travel over any obstacle or difficult terrain using four arms.

SPECIAL ABILITY: 4x4 Race

FAVOURITE GAME: Basket

SKILLS:

PROFILES

OH! 59

Loves to surprise all the other Gogo's.

SPECIAL ABILITY:
Hiding

FAVOURITE GAME: In Flight

SKILLS:

ALKALINE 60

Ultra turbo-charged power. Full blast energy.

SPECIAL ABILITY:
Battery Charger

FAVOURITE GAME: Battle

SKILLS:

PROFILES

61 AWA-SHIMA ♂

Always ready for action, but don't bother him for anything else.

SPECIAL ABILITY: Graffiti-Flash

FAVOURITE GAME: K.O.

SKILLS:

62 GHOST ♂

Dark mystery. Not everyone dares look him in the face.

SPECIAL ABILITY: Frightening Whisper

FAVOURITE GAME: Basket

SKILLS:

PROFILES

63 TUT

The curious mummy.
Can remove a tiny bit of bandage
to see what is going on.

SPECIAL ABILITY:
Healing

FAVOURITE GAME: K.O.

SKILLS:

MATSUE 64

Very proud of
his super-cool haircut.

SPECIAL ABILITY:
Soft Fringe

FAVOURITE GAME: In Flight

SKILLS:

CROSSWORD

Time to test your Gogo's Crazy Bone's knowledge. Do you know your Mosh from your Sato or your B-King from your Usuzi?

All the answers to this little puzzle can be found in this book, so even if you're not the world's biggest Gogo's brain, you still have a chance at being a champ.

ACROSS

1. All the Gogo's want to be his friend (4).
5. Don't stare into his eyes (6).
7. Gogo with the best sense of smell (4).
9. Very proud of his haircut (6).
11. The daring pirate Gogo (6)

DOWN

2. The game played by tossing Gogo's onto a line (2,4).
3. Absorbs pollution (6).
4. Loves music (3).
6. How many points a Gogo scores for standing up (4).
8. Likes to visit the swimming pool every day (3).
10. Not as grumpy as he looks (5).
11. The fastest Gogo (5).

TUBE'S TRIVIA

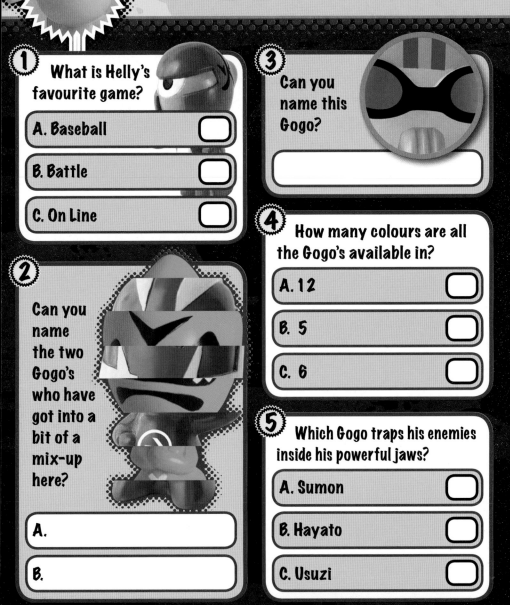

1 What is Helly's favourite game?

A. Baseball

B. Battle

C. On Line

2 Can you name the two Gogo's who have got into a bit of a mix-up here?

A.

B.

3 Can you name this Gogo?

4 How many colours are all the Gogo's available in?

A. 12

B. 5

C. 6

5 Which Gogo traps his enemies inside his powerful jaws?

A. Sumon

B. Hayato

C. Usuzi

FIND ALL THE ANSWERS ON PAGE 90 AND 91

PUZZLE CRAZY!

COLOUR MY GOGO®

We all know how colourful the Gogo's Crazy Bones gang are, but today seems to be a bit of a dull day for them. Use your pencils and pens to add some colour back to the picture below.

STADIUM SEARCH

PUZZLE CRAZY!

The Bones have had an invite to take part in the world's largest Gogo's Tournament Bash. In all their excitement they've lost the directions to the stadium.

Can you help them find their way to fame and glory?

START

FINISH

TOURNAMENT >

All the lights have gone out! The Gogo's Crazy Bones are needed for a match, but how are you supposed to choose which one to use when all you can see here are their shadows?

Time to put on your Gogo's detective hat and name the Gogo's you can see here before it's too late.

GOGO® GAME

4

5

7

6

67

FIND ALL THE ANSWERS ON PAGE 92

There's been a mix-up at the Gogo's factory and nobody knows how many Gogo's have been made today.

Take a look at the picture below and see if you can count how many of each Gogo appear in the pile of Bones waiting to be shipped out.

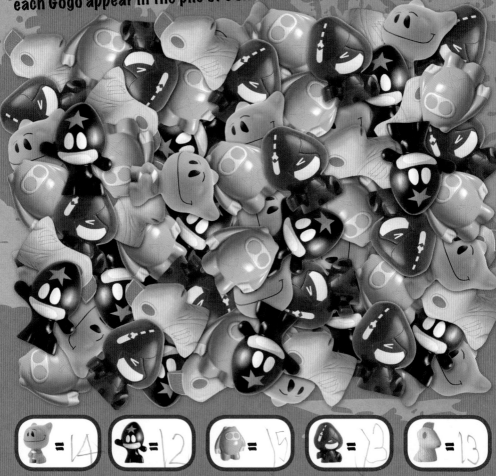

= 14   = 12   = 15   = 13   = 13

TUBE'S TRIVIA

1 He is mysterious and funny – who is he?

A. Okori

B. Skull

C. Pop

2

Can you name this mixed-up Gogo?

3

Can you name this Gogo?

4 Which Gogo loves music and dances non-stop?

A. Yuza

B. Kolo

C. Pop

5 Who has the special ability Wonder Nose?

A. Rufus

B. Raysun

C. Aiko

FIND ALL THE ANSWERS ON PAGE 92 AND 93

65 AKITA

Friend and loyal companion.
You can count on Akita.

SPECIAL ABILITY :
Antenna Horn

FAVOURITE GAME: On Line

SKILLS:

SHIZUOKA 66

With just one cry he can get the
attention of all the Gogo's.

SPECIAL ABILITY :
Gogo's Alert

FAVOURITE GAME: K.O.

SKILLS:

PROFILES

MIYAKE 67

Cuts through water at amazing speed.

SPECIAL ABILITY:
Rudder Shaped Crest

FAVOURITE GAME: On Line

SKILLS:

68 FUJICHIK

Flies fast and high, but lands soft and smooth.

SPECIAL ABILITY:
Instant Landing

FAVOURITE GAME: In Flight

SKILLS:

PROFILES

TSU 69

Juices, cold drinks,
he always has a drink handy.
A thirsty Gogo.

SPECIAL ABILITY:
Big Gulp

FAVOURITE GAME: Bowling

SKILLS:

---

70 **KOKUBU**

The life and soul of any party.
Invited to every occasion.

SPECIAL ABILITY:
Friend Visor

FAVOURITE GAME: Bowling

SKILLS:

PROFILES

IZUMI 71 ♂

Loves speed and never gets off his motorbike.

SPECIAL ABILITY:
Motorbike Racing

FAVOURITE GAME: On Line

SKILLS:

72 AKO ♂

The ultimate minder.
50 special moves ready to go.

SPECIAL ABILITY:
Martial Arts

FAVOURITE GAME: Battle

SKILLS:

PROFILES

KAMI-KAMI 73

Brushes his teeth before playing any game. Always fresh and minty.

SPECIAL ABILITY:
Super Bite

FAVOURITE GAME: Scoring

SKILLS:

SAGO 74

Changes shape to fit into any space.

SPECIAL ABILITY:
Self-Moulding

FAVOURITE GAME: Scoring

SKILLS:

PROFILES

VAMPA 75

Not seen much during the day.
He moves in the dark.

SPECIAL ABILITY:
Low-Level Flying

FAVOURITE GAME: Scoring

SKILLS:

76 MISHA

Cute and cuddly, the best
sleeping companion around.

SPECIAL ABILITY:
Makes You Sleepy

FAVOURITE GAME: Scoring

SKILLS:

77 YUZA

As strong as a rock.
Arms like granite.

SPECIAL ABILITY :
Weight Lifting

FAVOURITE GAME: K.O.

SKILLS:

TAN CHIA 78

Wants to be the Gogo's hero.
Always ready for action.

SPECIAL ABILITY :
Free Fighting

FAVOURITE GAME: Battle

SKILLS:

PROFILES

79 KOLO ♂

Futuristic Gogo who loves technology. Floats through space guided by the stars.

SPECIAL ABILITY:
Space Flight

FAVOURITE GAME: Bowling

SKILLS:

80 EVI ♂

Although it tries to frighten its friends, it makes them laugh more than anything.

SPECIAL ABILITY:
Attack of Laughter

FAVOURITE GAME: In Flight

SKILLS:

PUZZLE CRAZY!

DOODLE-

Time to test out your Gogo drawing skills. Can you copy the small image onto the larger box?

Use the grid for reference and when you are done, don't forget to add plenty of colour to your creation.

H-83
V

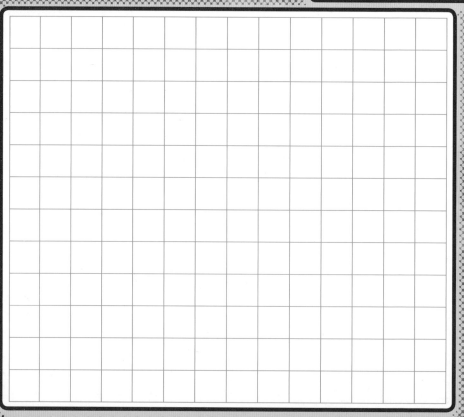

<CHIRO
V

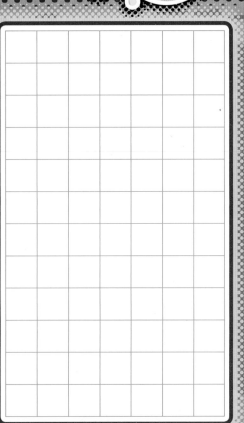

^
UFUS>

There's been a mix-up at the Gogo's Crazy Bones® headquarters and it seems that some of the Gogo's have had their names mixed up.

Can you figure out which name should actually go with which character. Use your Gogo's knowledge and the profiles in this book to put everything right.

1

SPEED

4

CROC

3

2

OKORI

5

SIMI

UMU

TUBE'S TRIVIA

1 Which Gogo wears this mask and why?

4 Which game does Hiro enjoy playing most?

A. Okori

B. Crazy Touch

C. In Flight

4 Which Gogo comes from Planet X?

A. Rufus

B. Lessi

C. Pop

4 Can you name this mixed-up Gogo?

3 He has a TV for a face. Can you name him?

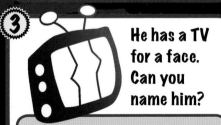

FIND ALL THE ANSWERS ON PAGE 92

Have you got all the Gogo's? This is a list of all the Gogo's Crazy Bones® available. Use it to keep track of the ones you've got and the ones you still need to collect.

01	MOSH		X		X		X		X
02	NASAKO		X		X		X		X
03	SATO		X		X		X		X
04	OKORI		X		X		X		X
05	TORI		X		X		X		X
06	HELLY		X		X		X		X
07	SKULL		X		X		X		X
08	ANGIRU		X		X		X	+08 S	X
09	UMU		X		X		X		X
10	AIKO		X		X		X		X

83

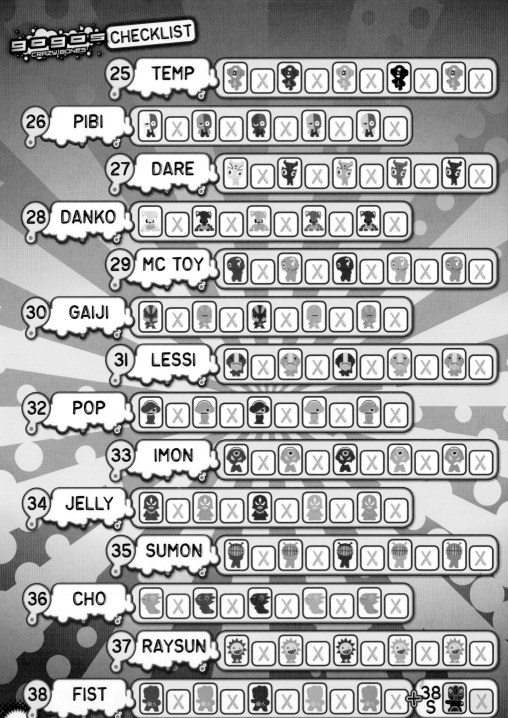

gogo's CRAZY BONES

CHECKLIST

No.	Name
25	TEMP
26	PIBI
27	DARE
28	DANKO
29	MC TOY
30	GAIJI
31	LESSI
32	POP
33	IMON
34	JELLY
35	SUMON
36	CHO
37	RAYSUN
38	FIST + 38 S

39 ZAR-ZAR ♂

40 HAYATO ♂

41 BIGU ♂

42 OJARU ♂

43 SPEED ♂

44 TREMI ♂

45 B-BOY ♂ +45 S

46 MOCHI ♂

47 POPUS ♂

48 TUBE ♂

49 CUBIC ♂

50 B-KING ♂

51 CROC ♂

52 UFUS ♂

67 MIYAKE ♂

68 FUJICHIK ♂

69 TSU ♂

70 KOKUBU ♂

71 IZUMI ♂

72 AKO ♂

73 KAMI KAMI ♂

74 SAGO ♂

75 VAMPA ♂

76 MISHA ♂

77 YUZA ♂

78 TAN CHIA ♂

79 KOLO ♂

80 EVI ♂

ANSWERS—ANSWERS

20 PUZZLE CRAZY! JIGSAW JUMBLE

21 TUBE'S TRIVIA

1. Ghost and Matsue
2. B. Double Fast Hook
3. A. Hiraku
4. Hiru
5. Raysun

32 PUZZLE CRAZY! PHOTO FOUL-UP

ANSWERS – ANSWERS

33 PUZZLE CRAZY! WACKY WORDS

B A Q Y
Z L T H N S L B S T
B F J I Q G L I O N S F
W U P J F X I A N K K W E F
C T G I M T P R S N O P O N E D
F L O A B R J Q U M S M E G R H A S
S D G F O C E I R O A L K A L I N E
K O T C I R S H O S S Q A W A D K R
D A M O L L Y S A S H I Z U O K A Q A S
A Y P L A S Y I T S I D K R S S V W K D
R M W A I K O C E W N M I D H S U X L G
E A S Q R I U O M I S H O T A O O L E A
H R C E N H E A L C C H H Z S Y T S
E I Y F C O R N I W O I W A O E S S
M T R L H U A N Y O O N U R S V I I
A A A E N A S A K O D O D I O H
N T K D S L T Y J E P C C L
L L U E I H D A R Q Q K
Y J R N J O R G R D
T U O U

47 TUBE'S TRIVIA

1. Hiraku
2. B. Cubic
3. B-Ball
4. Danko and Izumi
5. B. Lessi

ANSWERS—ANSWERS

53 TUBE'S TRIVIA

1. C. Codi
2. Matsue
3. Cho
4. Hiraku
5. B. Super Bite

62 PUZZLE CRAZY! CROSSWORD

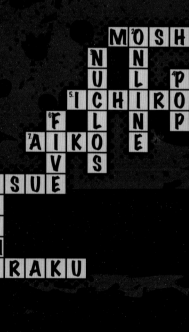

ANSWERS – ANSWERS

63 TUBE'S TRIVIA

1 C. On Line

2 Rufus and Gaiji

3 Izumi

4 B. 5

5 A. Sumon

65 PUZZLE CRAZY! STADIUM SEARCH

66 PUZZLE CRAZY! GUESS THE GOGO° GAME

1. Awa-Shima
2. Hiraku
3. Sumon
4.
5. Croc
6. Tube
7. Sun

68 PUZZLE CRAZY! COUNTING MAD

 =14 =12  =15 =13 =13

ANSWERS—ANSWERS

69 TUBE'S TRIVIA

3 Tremi

1 B. Skull

4 C. Pop

2 Tan Chia

5 C. Aiko

80 PUZZLE CRAZY! TITLE TROUBLE

1 Okori

2 Speed

3 Umu

4 Simi

5 Croc

81 TUBE'S TRIVIA

3 Codi

1 Nuclos – To reduce pollution

4 C. In Flight

2 Rufus

5 Neko

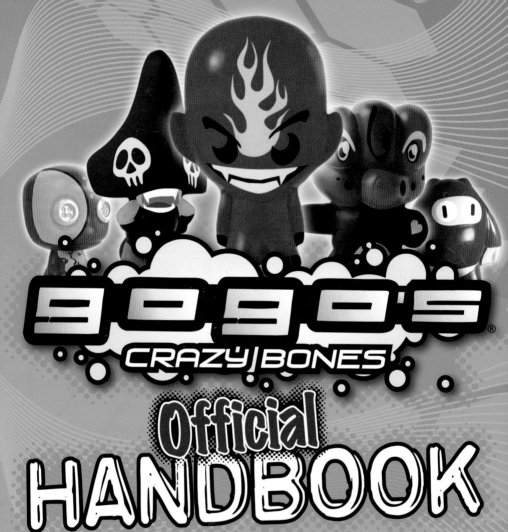

gogo's
CRAZY BONES

Official
HANDBOOK

GOGO'S CRAZY BONES® OFFICIAL HANDBOOK
A BANTAM BOOK 978 0 553 82093 5
First published in Great Britain by Bantam
an imprint of Random House Children's Books
A Random House Group Company
This edition published 2008
1 2 3 4 5 6 7 8 9 10
GOGO'S/CRAZY BONES © 2008 PPI - MARTOMAGIC, S.L.
Bantam Books are published by Random House Children's Books,
61-63 Uxbridge Road, London, W5 5SA
www.rbooks.co.uk
www.kidsatrandomhouse.co.uk
Addresses for companies within The Random House Group Limited can be found at:
www.randomhouse.co.uk/offices.htm
THE RANDOM HOUSE GROUP Limited Reg. No. 954009
A CIP catalogue record for this book is available from the British Library
Printed in Italy

MAGIC BOX INT.®

ppi Worldwide